A ROBOT WORLD

CLIVE GIFFORD

BARRON'S

© 2017 by Franklin Watts
An imprint of Hachette Children's Group
Part of the Watts Publishing Group
Carmelite House
50 Victoria Embankment
London EC4Y 0DZ
www.franklinwatts.co.uk
www.hachette.co.uk

Designer: Lisa Peacock
Editor: Nicola Edwards
Picture researcher: Kathy Lockley

Picture acknowledgments: The publisher would like to thank the following for permission to reproduce their pictures:
Alamy Stock Photo/REUTERS/Yuya Shino Cover; © American Honda Motor Co., Inc 30; The Australian Centre for Field Robotics
at the University of Sydney http://sydney.edu.au/acfr/agriculture 5 (bottom); Christoph Bartneck 57 (top left); CMU Field
Robotics Center 29 (bottom left); Compressorhead Rocks/ © Norman Konrad 46 (bottom), title page, / © David Medeiro—
heyjoeynyc 47 (bottom left); / © Martin Nicholas 46 (center left), 47 (top); Mark Richards, courtesy of the Computer History
Museum 14; CSA 24; Photo: Festo 5 (top); Courtesy of Flyability—www.flyability.com 29 (top left); © Frauenhofer IPA 37
(bottom right); Getty Images /BSIP/UIG via Getty 49 (top right), /JIJI PRESS/AFP 54–55, /Koichi Kamoshida/Staff 52–53,
/Patrick CHAPUIS/Gamma-Rapho via 28 (bottom), /Photo by Albert L. Ortega/WireImage 16 (right), /Photo by CBS via Getty,
17 (bottom left), /Photographer David Paul Morris/Bloomberg via Getty 15 (top right), /Photographer Nicky Loh/Bloomberg
via Getty 10, /STR/AFP 37 (center left), 41 (top right), /TOSHIFUMI KITAMURA/AFP 31(bottom center), 40–41 (bottom right),
42 (bottom), 43 (top); © 2017/Intuitive Surgical, Inc 34–35 (bottom right); JPL-Caltech 56 (top); Photo courtesy of Murata
Manufacturing Co., Ltd 56 (bottom); Musée d'art et d'histoire, Neuchâtel, Switzerland 7; NASA 4 (bottom), 25, 29 (bottom
right), (top right), 32 (bottom left), 32–33 (bottom left), 50–51; /JPL-Caltech/MSSS 51 (bottom right); National Oceanography
Centre 20 (top); Frederic Osada & Teddy Seguin/DRASSM 21 (top); REX/Shutterstock/ 17 (top), /MGM 17 (bottom right);
/Lucasfilm/20th Century Fox; 19 (top); Science Photo Library/Adam Hart-Davies 6 (right), /David Parker 13 (top left), /Sam
Ogden 22; SERBOT 36 (bottom right); Photo SERVA-TS 37 (top); Shutterstock.com 5 (center), 9 (bottom right), 26 (top), 26
(bottom), 31 (bottom right), 31 (bottom left), 31 (top), 35 (center), 35 (top right), 38 (top), 38 (bottom), 39, 47 (bottom right),
48–49, 53 (bottom right), 58 (bottom left), 59 (center), /Andrei Kholmov 12 (bottom), /Featureflash Photo Agency 18 (bottom
left), /Sarunyu L 19 (bottom), /SvedOliver 13 (top right); © Soft Bank Robotics 36 (left); TATRC 55 (top right); Wikipedia
Commons: 4 (center), 6 (left), 8, 9 (top right), 13 (bottom), 16 (left), 18–19, 21 (bottom right), 21 (bottom left), 22–23, 26–27,
27 (bottom), 42 (top), 43 (bottom left), 44–45, 49 (bottom right), 52 (bottom left), 53 (top right), 55 (bottom right), 57
(bottom left), 57 (top right), 58 (top), 59 (bottom), 59 (top left); /Alf van Beem 13 (bottom), /MattiPaavola 15 (bottom right),
/NASA 28 (top), /U.S. Army photo by Sgt. Kimberly Hackbarth, 4th SBCT, 2nd Inf. Div. Public Affairs Office 45 (top), /U.S. Navy
photo by Lithographer's Mate 1st Class John P. 20 (bottom); /U.S. Navy photo by Mass Communication Specialist 2nd Class
Jhi L. Scott/Released 44 (top), /With permission of Richard Greenhill and Hugo Elias 11.

Every attempt has been made to clear copyright. Should there be any inadvertent
omission, please apply to the publisher for rectification.

First edition for North America published in 2018 by
Barron's Educational Series, Inc.

All inquiries should be addressed to:
Barron's Educational Series, Inc.
250 Wireless Boulevard
Hauppauge, New York 11788
www.barronseduc.com

ISBN: 978-1-4380-5040-9

Library of Congress Control Number: 2017949412

Date of Manufacture: January 2018

Manufactured by: WKT Company Ltd., Shenzhen, China

Printed in China
9 8 7 6 5 4 3 2 1

CONTENTS

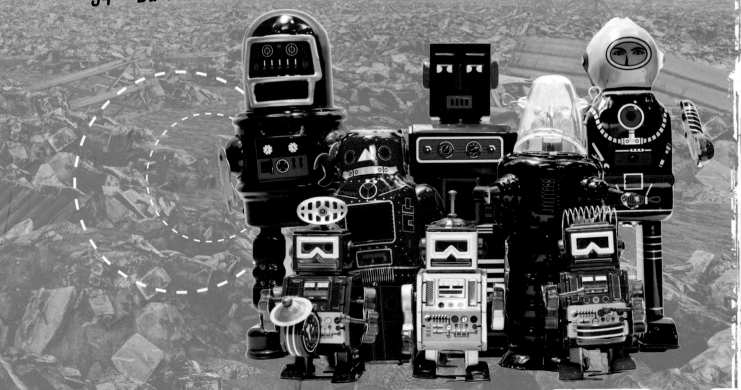

ROBOT PLANET

Robots are amazing, adaptable machines. Most can work without human help and many can perform tasks with more strength, precision, or stamina than people. From the first real robots of the twentieth century, robot numbers have boomed. They can now be found in action all over the world ... and beyond, in space.

USA

The *PR2* robot has two arms that can be programmed to perform many tasks. It's even been taught how to fold laundry and make the perfect coffee!

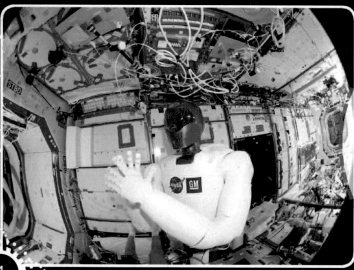

SPACE

Robonaut 2 is a two-armed humanoid robot sent into space to the International Space Station in 2011. It is a test bed for potential future humanoid space robots that may ease the workload of human astronauts.

GERMANY

Many mobile robots move around on wheels or tracks, but this Festo robot from Germany hops just like a kangaroo. It stores energy as it lands to help power its next hop of up to 3 ft (0.8 m).

JAPAN

Thousands of robots work in Japanese industry. Some, such as Nao (right) and Pepper (page 36), are found in banks, shops, and offices as guides and assistants.

AUSTRALIA

Robots are mostly found in factories and offices, but in Australia, some work on farms. Ladybird (shown here) is a solar-powered vegetable harvester, Rippa moves around fields, spraying weeds with weed killer, and Swagbot has been trained to herd cattle in the Australian outback.

AUTOMATA

In the past, people's fascination with machines extended to building lifelike mechanical figures that acted like humans or animals. These robots used springs, levers, gears, and other mechanical parts and were popularized by watch and clockmakers in Europe, the Middle East, and Asia.

DIGESTING DUCK

French watchmaker Jacques de Vaucanson built a remarkable digesting duck automaton in 1739. It contained 400 parts. The duck would flap its wings and stretch its neck to eat barley out of a human hand. Moments later it would excrete a dropping (made of pressed grass clippings) out of its rear.

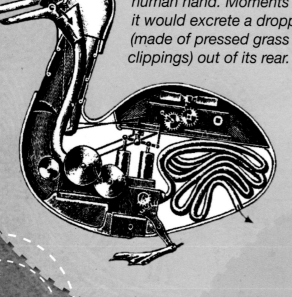

KARAKURI

In Japan, robots were made during the Edo period (1603–1868) and called *karakuri ningyo* (mechanical devices made to look like people). This Japanese Archer automaton from 1860 features an archer made of plaster with levers and gears of wood. Powered by a spring, the archer picks up and fires an arrow 10–13 ft (3–4 m) while the two women wave, clap, and ring a bell.

JAQUET-DROZ AUTOMATA

Swiss watchmaker Pierre Jaquet-Droz and his son, Henri-Louis, built some of the most complicated and lifelike human robots in the eighteenth century. These included The Writer (below/right) and The Lady Musician, made of 2,500 parts, which could move its fingers to play a keyboard instrument and curtsey when it finished playing.

THE WRITER

Designed in the early 1770s, The Writer is a model of a small boy sitting on a wooden stool. The model could handwrite messages in elegant script up to 40 characters long without any assistance.

HEAD

Gears inside the boy's head caused it to turn and its eyes to move as if reading the writing it produced.

INK POT

This pot contained real ink. The quill pen, made of a goose feather, was held in the robot's right hand and dipped into the pot before it handwrote each line.

PROGRAMMABLE DISC

Inside the figure, 40 mechanical parts on a large brass wheel could be altered to change the letters or characters handwritten by the figure. This made it one of the first ever programmable machines.

AWESOME ELEKTRO

In the 1920s and 1930s, engineers built a new generation of humanlike machines using mechanical and electrical parts to make them move, talk, and perform certain tasks. One of the most advanced of these machines was Elektro.

Built by US company Westinghouse, Elektro, a 7 ft (2.1 m) tall, 265 lb (120 kg) metal man, caused a sensation when it appeared at the 1939 World's Fair in New York.

CHEST

Electro's aluminum chest contained a telephone receiver and a lightbulb that flashed in response when someone spoke to the robot.

PET DOG

In 1940, Elektro was joined by a robotic pet dog called Sparko. Powered by two electric motors that drove gears and cables, Sparko could walk, sit, beg, and wag its tail.

EYES

The robot's eyes contained two light-sensitive devices called phototubes. These sent an electric signal when a particular color of light shined on them. They allowed Elektro to recognize two colors: green and red.

MOUTH

Elektro's mouth opened and closed when the robot spoke a few phrases such as, "My brain is bigger than yours!" These phrases were recorded in advance on 78 rpm records and played on a record player hidden nearby.

JOINTED FINGERS

Pulleys connected to electric motors allowed Elektro to move its fingers and sometimes grip small objects, such as a conductor's baton.

BRITAIN'S FIRST BOT

In 1928, Eric (above) was built by William H. Richards and Alan Reffell, mostly out of aluminum. The 99 lb (45 kg) robot could move its arms and turn its head. It went on a world tour before being scrapped. Eric was recreated for London's Science Museum's 2017 Robots exhibition.

FEET

Elektro didn't move its legs to walk in steps like most modern humanoid robots. Elektro traveled on four rollers under each of its 18 in (45 cm) long feet, powered by an electric motor.

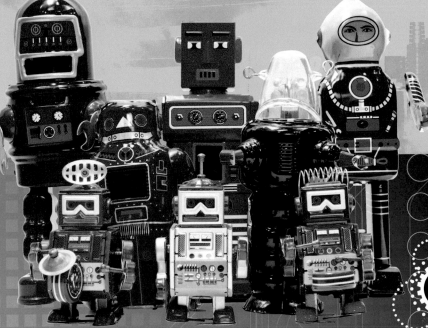

METAL MODELS

Metal model robots shaped like mechanical men became popular toys. These vintage models (right) date from the 1950s and 1960s.

BOT BASICS

Robots vary greatly in shape and size. Some are remote-controlled by people. Others are autonomous, which means they can work for long periods without human supervision. Baxter, built by Rethink Robotics in 2012, is a two-armed multipurpose robot for use in factories and research. It has many of the key parts that are found in all robots.

CONTROLLER

The controller is the processor or "brain" of the robot, usually a microprocessor chip or microcomputer. It keeps all the parts of the robot working together and makes decisions based on the data sent to it via the robot's parts and sensors. The controllers for some robots are located separately on a large computer and instruct the robots using wireless signals.

PROGRAMMING

Most controllers are reprogrammable so that the entire robot can be instructed to perform different sets of tasks. With some robots, this means writing programs on computers and uploading them to the machine. Baxter can be programmed simply by moving its hand to perform a task in the desired way.

SENSORS

These are devices—from light detectors to temperature measurers and camera-based vision systems—that gather information about the robot or its surroundings and send it back to the robot's controller. Contact sensors detect if part of the robot touches something, while proximity sensors measure the distances between the robot and nearby objects.

DRIVE SYSTEM

These are systems that transmit power to a robot to move its parts. Baxter's drive system, like that of many robots, is made up of a series of electric motors that move the joints in its arms and body. Some robots use pneumatic drive systems powered by air or other gases. Other robots use hydraulic systems, in which liquids in cylinders move rods, called pistons.

END EFFECTOR

Many robots have parts called end effectors that interact with their surroundings or handle objects. These might be scalpels and needles in a surgical robot or a drill, welding gun, or laser cutter in an industrial robot. Baxter can be fitted with different end effectors including a two-fingered gripper.

Each direction in which all or part of a robot can move is called a degree of freedom. The Shadow Dexterous Hand (right) is an advanced end effector. It has 20 degrees of freedom, enabling it to handle a wide range of objects and tools.

INDUSTRIAL ROBOTS

Robots make very productive workers, able to operate 24/7 in factories with just the occasional break for reprogramming or maintenance. From the very first, Unimate, in 1961, there are now over two million industrial robots hard at work.

UNIMATE

George Devol and Joseph Engelberger devised the two-ton Unimate robot to handle red hot metal car parts in a General Motors factory in Michigan, US. Unimate's steel arms and grippers could lift metal parts weighing up to 331 lb (150 kg). The robot performed 100,000 hours of work before being retired in 1971.

ROBOT ARMS

After the success of Unimate, industrial robot arms quickly developed to become versatile workers. Many have shoulder, elbow, and wrist joints similar to human arms. Sensors called joint encoders let the robot know the precise angle and position of each joint. These robots can be programmed to repeat the same task, such as spray painting a car, with perfect precision.

SPOT WELDING BOTS

Sparks fly as a robot welds a car body together, melting the car's metal to form a strong joint. A typical car may need 4,000 different welds, which a team of robots can manage accurately in just a few minutes.

QUICK PICKERS

This robot handles a glass car window safely using vacuum suckers to pick and place the glass. Many robots in factories pick and place objects for assembly or to package them up. The ABB 360-6 Flexpicker is one of the world's fastest—it can handle 400 objects per minute!

AGVS

Automated Guided Vehicles (AGVs), like this container mover at the Port of Rotterdam, Netherlands, are robotic fetchers and carriers. They are often programmed to follow set paths as they move parts and materials around. Some use their light sensors to follow bright lines painted on a factory floor.

SUPER SHAKEY

By the late 1960s, scientists were researching how robots on the move might find their own way around. The first mobile robot that could make decisions for itself was built at the Stanford Research Institute in the United States. It was named Shakey because it shook as it moved!

ON-BOARD LOGIC

Electronic circuits in Shakey's body translated commands from the computer into instructions to move or turn its wheels. When the robot was commanded to go to a particular place, it could work out, by itself, the best route to take.

CAT WHISKER WIRES

Long loops of wire acted as pioneering proximity sensors—devices that let Shakey know if it had bumped into something.

DRIVE WHEEL

Electric motors turned two drive wheels to move Shakey forward and back. The robot counted the turns of its wheels to work out how far it had traveled in one direction.

ANTENNA

Shakey used a two-way radio link to talk to the giant computer that controlled it. The computer's memory contained a map of all the laboratory rooms in which Shakey could move around.

RANGEFINDER

A beam of light from this device bounced off objects ahead to determine how far away they were. This helped Shakey steer around obstacles as well as identify and travel through doorways.

Today, mobile robots are used in large numbers. Amazon uses an amazing 15,000 Kiva robots to move packages around its warehouses automatically.

SPEEDING UP

Shakey was a pioneering robot, but it was slow—it could take over an hour to creep through a room. Later mobile robots, such as the Lynx office robot and this Justus inspection and security robot (right), could patrol large areas at much higher speeds.

ROBOT FRIENDS, ROBOT FOES

The first use of the term robot was in the 1921 play RUR (short for Rossum's Universal Robots) by the Czech writer Karel Capek. The humanlike machines in the play rebel against their human makers, a common theme in many films and TV shows ever since. Some fictional robots, though, are depicted as helpful and friendly allies of people.

USR NS-5

Starring in the 2004 movie, *I, Robot*, the NS-5 robots house powerful controllers able to make six trillion calculations every second. When a computer, V.I.K.I., uploads new software to each NS-5, the robots turn against their human masters.

TERMINATOR T-800

First seen as played by Arnold Schwarzenegger in the 1984 movie, the Cyberdyne Systems Model 101 Series 800 Terminator (known as the T-800) is a robot assassin sent back in time to kill the mother of the resistance leader, John Connor.

This lethal robot (right), its head and skeleton built of titanium, could run for 120 years on its power cells. Its piercing red eyes could be removed for repair and replacement.

K-9

The Fourth Doctor, played by Tom Baker in the UK TV show *Doctor Who*, was given a faithful and, sometimes heroic, sidekick in 1977. The robotic dog, originally called FIDO, became better known as K-9. Four versions of the robot starred in many different *Doctor Who* adventures and in its own TV show.

K-9's ear antennae could turn to locate intruders, while its nose held a hidden laser weapon. The model used in filming had four hidden wheels and was pulled around the studio on a piece of string!

DATA

Featured in *Star Trek: The Next Generation*, Data is an android built in the year 2335 that serves on-board the Enterprise starship. Despite possessing enormous computing power and artificial intelligence, Data struggles to understand human emotions and decisions as he remains a machine.

ROBBY THE ROBOT

First starring in the 1954 movie Forbidden Planet, this friendly fictional robot was featured in seven movies and more than a dozen TV series. More than 2,592 ft (790 m) of electrical wiring was required to create the robot's flashing lights, spinning antennae, and whirring machinery, much of it housed inside its clear, dome-shaped head.

17

R2-D2

Brave, cheeky, and resourceful, the droid mechanic R2-D2 has served many in the *Star Wars* movie series, including Padmé Amidala, Anakin Skywalker, and Luke Skywalker. The 3.6 ft (1.09 m) tall droid is a film icon and a favorite character among *Star Wars* fans.

TURNING HEADS

R2-D2's rotating, turret-shaped head houses cameras, a radar system that detects moving objects, a spotlight, and a retractable periscope.

ALL-TERRAIN TREADS

The droid moves around spacecrafts and over rough ground on its two all-terrain treads at the bottom of its legs. It has a third leg that can retract into its body.

Two R2-D2 models were used in the making of the first *Star Wars* movie—a remote-controlled version and one controlled from inside by actor Kenny Baker (above, left), who was 3.7 ft (1.12 m) tall.

HOLOPROJECTOR

This device enables R2-D2 to display realistic 3D movies of people or scenes, such as when the robot showed Obi-Wan Kenobi a holographic message from Princess Leia (right).

COMPUTER ACCESS

This computer interface arm (also known as a scomp link) allows R2-D2 to plug itself into computer systems to control them or gain important data from their memories.

R2-D2 was often in the thick of the action. In this scene, from the first Star Wars *movie, which was released in 1977, Princess Leia gives R2-D2 a holographic message.*

TOOLKIT

The robot's cylindrical body contains a variety of handy tools, including a fire extinguisher, extending tools and probes, as well as a series of rocket thrusters that allow it to blast away from danger.

POWER AND COMMUNICATION

The lower body contains R2-D2's recharger socket and a loudspeaker system that enables the droid to communicate with a series of whirrs and beeps.

Making its debut in the movie Star Wars: The Force Awakens *was a successor to R2-D2 called BB-8. This robot rolls around on its ball-shaped body as it helps its owner Poe Dameron, an X-Wing fighter pilot.*

19

UNDERWATER ROBOTS

Working underwater is difficult for humans, so some robots have been built to take the strain. Underwater bots can scour the seabed for new features, examine underwater life close-up, or help recover ship and plane wrecks.

UNDER THE ICE

Some underwater robots travel long distances as they explore the ocean floor and monitor seawater and sea life. In 2009, Autosub 3 (above) dived beneath 1,640 ft (500 m) of solid ice and traveled 68 mi (110 km) as it explored Antarctica's ice shelves. It was powered by 5,000 D-cell torch batteries.

ROBOT RESCUER

A Scorpio robot (shown here being loaded onto an aircraft) freed an AS-28 submersible trapped on the Arctic Ocean floor in 2005, saving the lives of seven crew members.

TREASURE HUNTERS

Underwater robots have found shipwrecks and recovered treasures from their remains. In 2007, for example, Odyssey robots recovered 600,000 silver coins from a secret wreck in the Atlantic Ocean. An earlier robot, Jason Jr., explored the wreck of the *RMS Titanic* in 1986.

Stanford University's OceanOne (below) is a two-armed deep-diver robot that humans can control from the surface. In 2016, it explored the wreck of a 350-year-old French warship, found 328 ft (100 m) deep on the Mediterranean Seabed.

Robot hands can adjust grip force so they don't damage delicate objects.

Twin cameras provide 3D vision.

Eight small thrusters move the robot through the water.

COPYING NATURE

Most underwater robots are powered by electric motors turning propellers. Some robots, such as Robopike (below, right) and RoboTuna are modeled on how fish swim to provide more efficient ways of traveling through water. Other robots, like Cryo, are shaped and swim like jellyfish!

DEEP DIVERS

Water pressure increases sharply the deeper you dive. Beyond a certain depth, the pressure is so great it can crush a submarine like a tin can. Sturdy robots, like Nereus (above, left) and Kaiko, have traveled to the deepest part of Earth's oceans, around 36,089 ft (11,000 m) below sea level.

KISMET

Built at the Massachusetts Institute of Technology (MIT) in 1997, Kismet was a pioneering robot head which could interact with people. Based on what it saw or heard, it could respond with one of nine facial expressions: fear, acceptance, fatigue, contentment, sternness, disgust, anger, surprise, and sadness.

EXPRESSIVE EARS

The robot's ears can perk up to show attention or fold back to look angry. If Kismet senses a person is present, it can try to grab their attention by waggling its ears.

MEET ITS MAKER

Cynthia Breazeal became fascinated by robots, especially R2-D2, when she first watched Star Wars at the age of eight. She has built many sociable robots since, including Kismet, Nexi, and Jibo, and is now director of the Personal Robots Group at MIT.

MOVING MOUTH

Kismet can open and close its mouth. Its lips are powered by four small electric actuators. These can curl the lips upward for a smile or downward for a grimace or frown.

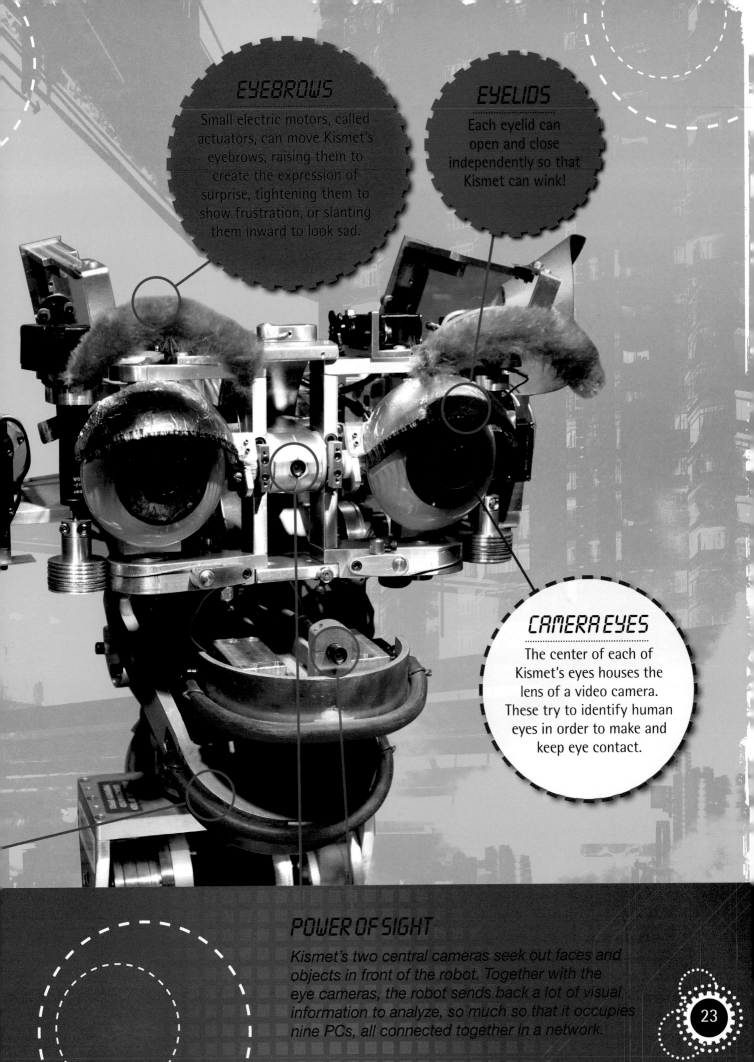

EYEBROWS

Small electric motors, called actuators, can move Kismet's eyebrows, raising them to create the expression of surprise, tightening them to show frustration, or slanting them inward to look sad.

EYELIDS

Each eyelid can open and close independently so that Kismet can wink!

CAMERA EYES

The center of each of Kismet's eyes houses the lens of a video camera. These try to identify human eyes in order to make and keep eye contact.

POWER OF SIGHT

Kismet's two central cameras seek out faces and objects in front of the robot. Together with the eye cameras, the robot sends back a lot of visual information to analyze, so much so that it occupies nine PCs, all connected together in a network.

CANADARM2

A giant robot arm, Canadarm2, left Earth in 2001 on-board the space shuttle Endeavour, bound for the fledgling International Space Station (ISS). Since then it has helped to build the space station, moving modules and parts around and even capturing visiting unmanned spacecraft that are bringing supplies and parts from Earth.

MOBILE BASE

The arm can attach itself to the Mobile Remote Service Base System fixed to the main frame of the ISS. The base can slide along the frame on rails to move Canadarm2 almost the entire length of the space station.

WRIST JOINT

This can move in three different directions, just like a human wrist.

LATCHING END EFFECTOR (LEE)

At each end of the arm there's a Latching End Effector (LEE). These can attach onto certain points of the space station's frame or be fitted with devices to capture visiting spacecraft. Astronauts can even ride the robot arm using a platform with foot restraints fitted to the LEE.

ELBOW JOINT

The robotic arm has seven joints, allowing the two main arm booms to bend. On either side of these joints are two color TV cameras that send back signals to astronauts inside the ISS.

DEXTRE

Arriving at the ISS in 2008, this twin-armed robot turns at its waist and can be attached to Canadarm2 for complex tasks, such as replacing a power module, fitting an antenna, or moving external storage containers around the space station.

SELF-REPAIRING

In 2014, Canadarm2 became the first robot in space to help repair itself. Working with Dextre, the robot arm removed and replaced a faulty video camera on one of its elbow joints with a new one.

OPTIMUS PRIME

Transformer toys were launched in Japan in 1984 with the slogan "Robots in Disguise." Their success inspired a cartoon series, computer games, books, feature-length movies, and many generations of toys and models.

HEROIC HUMANOIDS

The Transformers' home is the fictional planet Cybertron, where Optimus Prime is the leader of the Autobots (humanoid robots that transform into vehicles). The Autobots battle the evil Decepticons, led by the powerful and cunning Megatron (right).

SHAPE SHIFTER

Like all Transformers, Optimus Prime can change from a robot to another object, in this case a powerful truck. Optimus Prime toys boast intricate designs with lots of hinged and folding parts to transform between robot and vehicle.

LEGS

These contain sets of wheels that, when the legs fold back during transformation, become the truck wheels.

SHOULDERS

Powerful shoulders are fitted with smoke stacks that become the truck's exhausts when Optimus Prime transforms.

BARRAGE CANNONS

In some Optimus Prime versions, the robot is equipped with lethal barrage cannons that can fire warheads long distances. In truck mode, these act as rocket boosters for a powerful injection of speed.

ARMED ARMS

The robot's arms contain two swords, known as battle blades. They are charged before use to glow red hot at temperatures of up to 1,000°F (538°C). Two hooks, made from the fictional element Energon, can also appear from the robot's wrists.

ROBOT EXPLORERS

Robots are sent to places that are difficult or dangerous for people to visit. They provide ways of exploring areas on land, underwater, or in space without risking human life.

SPACE ROVERS

In 1970, the first space rover, Lunokhod I (right), traveled across the Moon on its eight wheels for 322 days, remote-controlled from Earth. It sent back more than 20,000 photographs.

ROBOTIC ARCHAEOLOGY

Small robots can travel through narrow stone passageways to reveal ancient wonders. In 2005, a robot was inserted into a narrow stone tunnel in the ancient Egyptian Pyramid of Khufu (right). Small mobile rovers can explore the interior of ancient structures and make discoveries.

iRobot

DRONES AND DANGER

Remote-controlled drones can be sent to explore isolated or dangerous areas. One drone with a difference is the twin-propeller-driven Gimbal (below) built by Flyability. It has explored hazardous ice caves in glaciers encased in an iron cage that protects the drone should it crash.

SNAKEBOTS

Robots made up of many small sections all jointed together (above) can slither their way through narrow passages and channels. These snakebots can be fitted with micro cameras to send back images of what they discover.

VOLCANOBOTS

Few places are more dangerous than the crater of an active volcano. Yet, in 1994, the Dante II robot (left) used its eight legs to clamber down into the vent of Mount Spurr in Alaska to gather gas samples. Twenty years later, NASA's two-wheeled VolcanoBots (below) explored volcanoes on the Hawaiian islands.

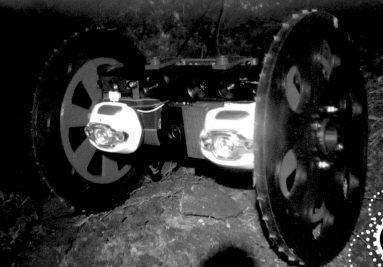

THE AMAZING ASIMO

Humanoid robots moved slowly and unsteadily until the arrival of Honda's ASIMO robot in 2000. Constantly tinkered with since, the 4 ft (1.3 m) tall robot is one of the most mobile and versatile humanoid robots around.

JOINTS

ASIMO has hip, knee, and ankle joints to give it great freedom of movement.

FEET

These are wide to give a stable grip when standing on one leg. Each foot contains force sensors that measure the amount of impact with the ground. They allow the robot to adjust its foot and leg movements when walking over uneven surfaces.

HEAD

This contains two cameras linked to the robot's controller, which can recognize up to ten human faces and track movement of people and objects in front of the robot.

BACKPACK

This houses the computers that control the robot's movement. Unlike many humanoids, ASIMO can move toward its target, turn and shift direction without stopping to think. Based on the next movements its legs will make, ASIMO shifts its body angle to keep itself balanced as it moves.

BODY

It keeps the weight down to five to one-half, ASIMO's body is a lightweight magnesium metal frame covered in plastic panels.

HONDA

HANDS

Featuring jointed fingers and a strong wrist joint powered by an electric motor, these allow the robot to grip objects, twist and open bottles, and even be programmed to perform sign language or conduct an orchestra.

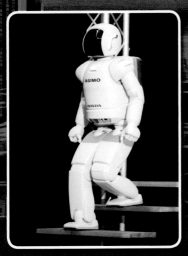

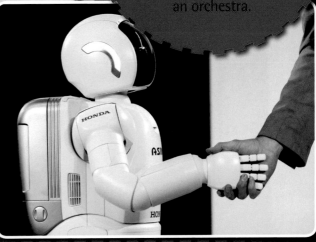

Bipedal (two-legged) robots often struggle with their balance when they move, but not ASIMO. It can run 6 mph (9 km/h) and climb and descend stairs with ease. It can also jog backward, jump, and hop.

GLOBAL HAWK

Unmanned Aerial Vehicles (UAVs) are pilotless flying robots. Some are drones, flown constantly by a human using a remote control. Global Hawk, though, can fly itself without any human help for long periods. All it needs is a mission plan programmed into its flight computers.

SATELLITE LINK

Located in the bulbous nose is a large dish antenna, 47 in (120 cm) in diameter. This enables the UAV to send images, and other information it collects, back to base via radio waves.

DRYDEN FLIGHT RESEARCH CENTER

ON THE GROUND

In a "Mission Control Element," human crew members monitor a Global Hawk flight using their computer screens. The screens display details about the robot, its position, and the information it is sending back. The crew can alter the robot's flight path using a keyboard and mouse.

ENGINE

The robot's single turbofan jet engine burns a mixture of fuel and air to create rapidly inflating gases. As the gases expand out of the back of the engine, they propel the flying robot forward at a top speed of 391 mph (629 km/h).

V-SHAPED TAIL

Global Hawk's two tail fins contain hinged panels at the rear that the on-board computers can instruct to move, helping the UAV to turn in the sky.

COMPUTER CONTROL

Global Hawk's 48 ft (14.5 m) long body houses its electronics and two flight computers that control the UAV's movements, keeping track of its position all the time.

872

NASA

OP GRUMMAN

NASA

FUEL TANKS

Tanks in the wings and body can carry up to 171 lb (7,847 kg) of fuel, giving the robot more than 30 hours' flying time.

CHASING HURRICANES

Global Hawk can fly at altitudes of up to 60,000 ft (18,288 m)—almost twice the altitude of a jet airliner. NASA uses two Global Hawks to fly above hurricanes to measure them and track their paths.

DA VINCI

Some robots carry bed linen, medicine, and other supplies around hospitals. Others, like the da Vinci robot, work at the sharp end, assisting human surgeons during operations. These robots help perform keyhole surgery, during which a small cut is made in the patient's body to allow microsurgery to be done.

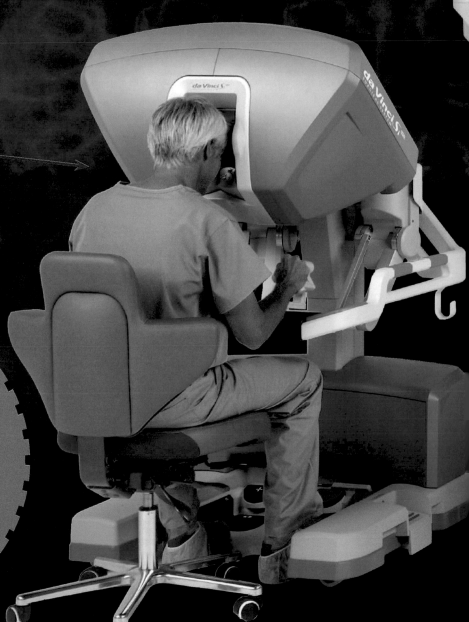

SURGEON CONSOLES

A human surgeon sits at this unit, viewing 3D, high-resolution images of the operation.

KEYHOLE SURGERY

The surgeon holds the master controls. As he or she moves them, signals are sent to the robot's arms to instruct them how to move and work. The robot arms are capable of incredibly precise movement, more accurate than a person's hand, and without the hand tremor (shaking) that affects humans.

PATIENT CART

Positioned alongside the patient during an operation, the patient cart features four robot arms. Three of these are fitted with a highly flexible EndoWrist joint that has seven degrees of freedom and can hold various surgical tools.

ENDOSCOPIC STACK

This tower includes a large screen that displays the operation to staff in the operating theater. It receives images from inside the patient taken by the tiny video camera fitted to da Vinci's fourth robot arm.

SURGICAL SHIELDS

During surgery, the entire robot is shrouded in covers to keep the operation area free of germs. More than three million operations have been performed by these robots, built by Intuitive Surgical.

ROBOT TOOLS

The tools used by the robot include forceps, sharp scalpels, knot-tying fine grippers, and lasers that cauterise (burn) a small part of the body, such as a blood vessel, to remove or seal it.

SERVICE ROBOTS

More and more robots are working in public areas including hotels, shops, and even parks, where robots mow the grass as they navigate around obstacles. What other robots are at our service?

GREETERS AND GUIDES

A number of social robots, from Pepper (left) in Carrefour stores in France to Ati in a museum in South Korea, are used to welcome people, guide them around and answer their questions. Some, such as the Beam Pro robots found at San Francisco's de Young Museum, can be instructed from the Internet, using their video cameras as they move around the museum to give people at home a remote tour.

CLEAN MACHINES

Window cleaning robots can operate on the glass walls of skyscrapers or move up steep slopes to clean large solar panels, using vacuum suction to stay in place. The Serbot Gekko robot (above, right) can clean up to 4,306 sq ft (400 sq m) per hour—that's 10-15 times what a human window cleaner could manage.

PARKING ROBOTS

A large self-driving robotic forklift, called Ray, parks cars in tight spaces at Düsseldorf Airport. It scans vehicles with lasers to learn their precise size and can fit over 1½ times as many cars in the facility than if humans parked them. What's more, the robot can connect to the airport's flight arrival computers to have each vehicle ready for its owner on his/her return.

ROBOTIC RESTAURANTS

Robot bartenders, cooks and waiters are becoming a reality, especially in China. One restaurant in the Chinese city of Harbin employs more than 20 robots. Some of them work in the kitchens, cooking noodles and deep frying dishes, while others carry meals on trays to diners at tables (above).

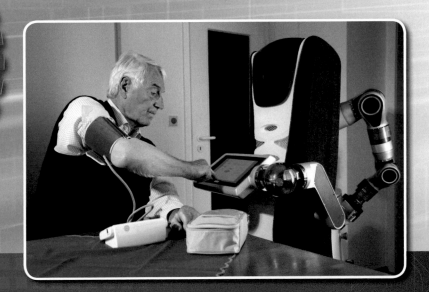

CARING BOTS

A number of robots are being developed to assist and care for elderly people. Care-O-Bots 3 and 4 are able to fetch and carry items, open doors, and communicate with a person via a screen. They can also send back results of medical checks, such as this blood pressure measurement (above, right), to a doctor or hospital.

WALL-E

Who would have thought that a fictional 700-year-old garbage-handling robot would become a movie star? But the inquisitive Waste Allocation Load Lifter Earth-Class (WALL-E) proved an engaging and popular title character of the smash-hit animated movie by Pixar in 2008.

A GARBAGE TALE

The movie tells the story of WALL-E, the last working robot on Earth, showing it sorting and stacking garbage, even though all the humans have left the planet. WALL-E becomes fond of a visiting space probe called EVE (below, right) and ends up in space trying to save EVE and itself.

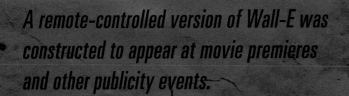

A remote-controlled version of Wall-E was constructed to appear at movie premieres and other publicity events.

LASER CUTTER

WALL-E uses a high-powered laser to cut up large pieces of metal waste. Lasers are concentrated narrow beams of light used in real life for cutting, etching, surgery, and for measuring long distances accurately.

SHOVEL HANDS

The robot uses its three-fingered shovel hands to dig holes quickly and to handle all sorts of objects, from a delicate plant seedling to a fire extinguisher. When sleeping or hiding, WALL-E retracts its arms, tracks, and head into its box-shaped body.

VISION SYSTEM

WALL-E's two large camera eyes can zoom in on objects in the distance. A sensor detects dust storms while they are still far away, allowing the robot to seek shelter.

ON TRACK

WALL-E runs on short tracks that enable it to clamber over piles of garbage and rough ground. The robot recharges its batteries using solar panels that fold out from its chest.

CHEST CRUSHER

The front of the robot contains a strong trash compactor. This crushes and presses garbage into cubes that WALL-E can then stack into tall piles.

TMSUK ENRYU

The T-52 Enryu—Japanese for "rescue dragon"—was built by Tmsuk in 2004. This 11 ft (3.45 m) tall robot towers over people and looks fearsome, but was actually designed to be a lifesaver—clearing debris and rescuing people trapped after a disaster.

GIANT ARMS

Each of Enryu's two arms is 20 ft (6 m) long. The arms are powered by a hydraulics system that uses oil under pressure in cylinders. This gives the robot awesome power—each arm can lift weights of up to 1,102 lb (500 kg).

BULLDOZER BLADE

The blade at the front can push away snow or mud as it rumbles forward at a top speed of 2 mph (3 km/h), powered by its diesel engine.

ALL-TERRAIN TRACKS

The five-ton robot runs on crawler tracks. These allow it to travel over rubble and across soft ground.

DIGITAL CAMERAS

The robot carries nine CCD digital cameras mounted on its head, body, and arms. These use radio signals to send back views of the scene to human rescue workers who may be some distance away.

POWERFUL GRIPPERS

Large steel grippers on the end of Enryu's arms can tilt a car on its side or grip and rip a car door off to let rescue workers get to injured passengers inside.

COCKPIT AREA

A human can stand inside the robot and operate it directly using hand controls. The robot can also be controlled from a distance, using a set of joysticks.

LITTLE BROTHER

Tmsuk developed a successor to T-52, the T-53, which still weighs three tons, but is smaller and able to maneuver in smaller spaces. The T-53 was used to help clear rubble and debris after an earthquake struck the Japanese city of Kashiwazaki in 2007.

ROBOT PETS

Robot pets started out as fun toys for children. As more sensors and computing power were added, many models started to be used by adults, too. Today's robot pets act as companions for the elderly or sick, as learning or caring aids, or even as security monitors when people are away from home.

Designed as a toy, the Tekno Newborn Kitty responds to voice commands to sit, beg, and even to jump into your hand.

ROBOT PAL

Devices like Sega's Dream Cat Venus, Omron's Tama cat, and the Japanese seal robot Paro are built to provide companions for the elderly. The robots' touch sensors let them respond to strokes and cuddles with sounds and movements, making their owners feel less lonely, but without the fuss of keeping a real pet. The pet AI that robotic pets need is in charge of their activities once at work.

GOOD DOG!

Sony's AIBO ERS-7 robotic dogs are able to recognize friendly faces and voices, play with a ball, and fetch objects. When its power is low, the robot automatically finds and sits down on its energy station to recharge its battery. Some AIBOs have been programmed to play soccer at RoboCup competitions (see page 49).

Face lights up when AIBO recognizes a familiar person. The tail may also wag. Touch sensors along its back and head register a stroke with a happy response.

Video camera in snout takes images and sends them wirelessly to the owner's computer.

The body houses a memory stick that can be loaded with new programs and modes. These allow AIBO to play games or act as a security guard, detecting unexpected movement or sounds, taking photos and sending them to its owner's email account.

Pressure sensors in the paws judge whether the dog is walking on a hard or soft surface to help it grip.

DINOPET

Robot pets aren't just cats and dogs. Pleo (left) and its successor Pleo rb are dinosaur pets that go through four stages of life, from infant to adult. As they mature, they develop new skills and parts of their personality.

A temperature sensor in Pleo causes it to shake and sneeze if its surroundings are cold, or pant and appear dizzy if it is too hot.

PACKBOT

The 510 Packbot is the world's most common military robot. Over 4,500 have been built. In under two minutes, the robot can be powered up and set to work, investigating bombs and booby traps, handling hazardous materials, or scouting buildings or war zones for dangers ahead.

MANIPULATOR ARM

The 74 in (187 cm) long manipulator arm has eight degrees of freedom and can bend to work around corners.

FLIPPERS

Two tracked flippers can rotate down and position themselves underneath the robot to lift it up and over an obstacle, or to flip it over if it has fallen and landed on its back. They can also help the robot climb stairs.

RUBBER TRACKS

The 27 in (68.6 cm) long robot (with flippers tucked away) is small enough to fit in the trunk of a car or a jeep, or even a soldier's backpack. It is powered by electric motors. Its ridged caterpillar tracks can grip soft ground and travel up slopes up to 60 degrees steep.

DRIVE CAMERA

One of up to four cameras found on the robot, the drive camera can tilt upward to give a close-up view of the gripper or point forward and turn from side to side to show the view ahead.

SURVEILLANCE CAMERA

This high-resolution camera has a 300x zoom to provide human personnel with a detailed view around corners or inside a suspicious vehicle.

Packbot's arm can be fitted with different tools, including cable cutters, car window glass breakers, and water disrupters. These fire a powerful blast of water into a suspected bomb to destroy its circuits before it can detonate and explode.

RADIO ANTENNAS

Stream images taken by the robot's cameras, and data from other sensors, are sent back to humans at a safe distance of up to 3,281 ft (1,000 m) away.

CHASSIS BED

The space between the two tracks can be filled with different instruments such as devices that measure harmful radiation. In 2011, Packbots were the first robots to enter and investigate the Fukushima nuclear power station in Japan after it had been devastated by an earthquake.

COMPRESSORHEAD

Built from scrap vehicle and machine parts, Compressorhead has to be the ultimate heavy metal band! The three-piece, all-robot band played their first gig in 2013 and have wowed large festival audiences. A YouTube video of one of their performances has received over 7.1 million views.

AIR GUITAR

The builders of the robots used pneumatics to power the robots' moving parts. Compressed air moves rods, called pistons, up and down a cylinder. Large pneumatic cylinders allow Fingers, for example (below, left), to rise and fall in time with the music.

FINGERS

Compressorhead's guitarist, Fingers, is aptly named. It has a total of 78 fingers, which it uses to strum or pick the strings of its Gibson Flying V guitar. Each of the robots is controlled by signals from a different laptop computer using a Musical Instrument Digital Interface (MIDI) to instruct the robot what to play.

BONES

Built in 2012, the band's bass player has just four thick fingers on each of its two robotic hands. The jointed fingers of its left hand press down on the strings along the neck of its Fender Precision bass guitar to play the different bass notes.

STICKBOY

Compressorhead's drummer is a gifted player, aided by its four arms, each holding a drumstick. Its foot plays the bass drum. As Stickboy beats the 14-piece drum kit, its head nods in time with the music.

ROBOT RIVALS

Compressorhead may be the hardest-rocking robots, but there are other robot musicians, too. In 2005, Toyota unveiled its Partner Robots, one of which (right) could be programmed to play simple tunes on a violin.

NAO

Small but smart, the NAO humanoid robot stands just 23 in (58 cm) tall and weighs a mere 12 lb (5.4 kg), but packs a powerful punch. Developed since 2004, these robots are versatile and fully programmable using a range of different computer languages and tools. More than 9,000 are in use around the world.

GRIPPING HANDS

Two fingers on each hand have small touch sensors and can be programmed to grip objects when they come within their grasp.

JOINTS

Fourteen electric motors power the robot's leg, arm, and head joints, enabling it to move with 25 degrees of freedom and pose in almost any position. An electronic device in its body enables the robot to keep its balance as it moves.

FOOT BUMPERS

The front of each foot contains simple touch sensors that switch on when the foot comes into contact with an object.

MICROPHONES

NAO's microphones pick up sounds and speech. The robot can understand speech and translate text to speech in 19 different languages, including Arabic, Chinese, and Spanish.

TWIN CAMERAS

Mounted in the middle of its face, NAO's cameras send images back to its controller to help it recognize shapes, objects, and gestures. It also knows its owner's face and greets him/her by name.

IN THE CLASSROOM

NAO robots let long-term ill children keep in touch with their classmates and lessons as part of the European Avatar Kids project. The NAO robot stands in for the child in class and relays video and sound back to the child, who can control the robot from the hospital using a computer tablet.

FUN AND GAMES

Troops of NAO robots have been taught how to perform dance routines, showcase beatbox tracks using their loudspeakers, and play soccer as a team. The B-Human team of NAO soccer-playing robots won RoboCup 2016 in Leipzig, Germany.

MARS CURIOSITY ROVER

The largest robot to move on Mars, NASA's Curiosity Rover is the size of a small car and weighs 1,982 lb (899 kg). The first robot rover on Mars, Sojourner, weighed just 24 lb (11 kg). Curiosity is packed with scientific instruments to explore the planet's climate and geology.

MONITORING

This mini weather station records wind speed, humidity, temperature, and pressure of the planet's atmosphere.

WHEELS

Six aluminum wheels, each 20 in (50 cm) in diameter, are fitted with small studs for grip and powered by their own electric motor. With its wheels mounted on movable legs, the rover can clear large rocks and stay stable at angles of up to 45°.

SCIENCE LAB

Rock samples are analyzed inside the robot's body to check for evidence as to whether there has ever been life on Mars.

CHEMCAM

This scientific instrument fires a narrow laser to vaporize (turn solids into gases) a small sample of Martian rock. The rest of the instrument can then identify whether any chemicals vital to life, such as oxygen, carbon, and hydrogen, are present.

ROBOT HAND

Located at the end of the 7 ft (2.1 m) long arm is a collection of tools, including a soil scoop, a brush to remove dust, and a drill that can bore 2 in (5 cm) deep holes to collect samples.

MASTCAM

A pair of high-resolution color cameras can take 3D photos. Over 10 years in action, they have the Curiosity rover sent back over 30,000 images, including the first selfie taken on Mars.

PLUTONIUM POWER SUPPLY

The rover's two large batteries are recharged by a generator. This is powered by heat from 11 lb (4.8 kg) of radioactive plutonium dioxide, enough for 14 years of operation.

51

LEARNING WITH ROBOTS

Many robots are found in classrooms and labs. Here, people learn about robotics and how these machines can be programmed to act and react to their surroundings.

LEGO MINDSTORMS

The popular kit robots have been through three generations since their launch in 1998. Users can construct their own robotic machines (right) using LEGO bricks and parts including motors, sensors, and a programmable controller.

SERVO

These small electric motors are powered by the robot's battery pack and can move the robot's movable parts such as its legs, gripping claw, or hands.

EDUBOTS

Robots for education and to build as a hobby first emerged in the 1980s, with machines including the Androbot Topo, GRC's RB5X, and the Heathkit Hero Jr. Modern educational robots range from simple kits, such as Cybot or Arduino, to sophisticated humanoid robots such as NAO (see pages 48–49) and DARwIn-OP (above).

ULTRASONIC SENSOR

This sensor block measures distances between 1 in (3 cm) and 92 in (233 cm) by sending out sound signals and calculating how long they take to bounce back off objects.

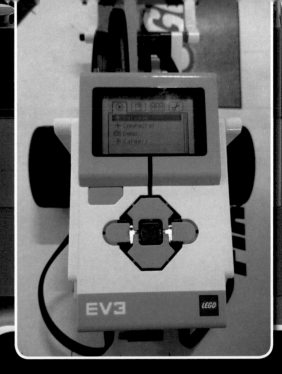

MICROCOMPUTER

The microcomputer inside this large brick acts as the robot's controller, instructing all its parts. The controller can be programmed using a range of computer languages. On the bottom it has six sockets to connect sensors and other devices to the controller.

POWERFUL CONTROLLER

The EV3 is LEGO Mindstorms' latest and most powerful controller brick. It was used to build the CubeStormer III robot, which holds the world record for solving a Rubik's cube in just 3.26 seconds!

TOUCH SENSOR

This sensor sends a signal to the controller letting it know whether it has been bumped, is being pressed down, or has just been released. The two arrow buttons and orange button on the RCX controller can also be programmed to act as touch sensors.

IN COMPETITION

Schools and hobby groups often build robots to take part in competitions. This Mindstorms robot (above) competed in a Bulgarian school's competition in 2016, and was equipped with light sensors to follow a curving black line.

ROBEAR

Robots are being developed that will help patients in hospitals and injured troops and personnel out in the field. ROBEAR was built by the Riken Institute in Japan and is designed to lift patients in and out of beds and wheelchairs in hospitals and care homes.

HEAD

Styled to look like a friendly polar bear cub to reassure patients, ROBEAR's head contains cameras and other sensors. These help measure the distances to a patient and his/her bed or wheelchair. The robot is controlled by people, either by touching the robot's arms to tell it to move or, wirelessly, using an Android tablet as the controller.

BODY

ROBEAR's body contains a microphone for receiving verbal instructions from a human controller and a bundle of lithium-ion batteries. These give the prototype robot a working time of about four hours before it needs recharging.

BASE

The robot moves on wheels fitted underneath its wide base. The extending legs in the base spread the weight of the 309 lb (140 kg) robot and any load it might be carrying so that ROBEAR doesn't topple over when it leans forward. The legs of the base can telescope inward to save space when the robot isn't being used.

HIGH-TECH HELPERS

Caregivers lift patients in and out of beds or wheelchairs an average of 40 times a day, putting great strain on their backs. So, robots, which could do the lifting for them under their guidance, would be a great help.

PADDED ARMS

Soft arm bumpers made of rubber foam provide cushioning as the robot lifts a patient up or down. ROBEAR can lift up to 176 lb (80 kg) in weight. The arms' electric motors move slowly and accurately to handle the patient comfortably. Sensors in the arms weigh each patient to calculate how much force to use to lift him/her.

BEAR

The Battlefield Extraction Assist Robot (BEAR) is an American prototype robot designed to pick up and rescue injured troops using its large paddles like a forklift. BEAR can travel across rough ground, steep slopes, and even clamber up stairs on its rugged tracks.

LS3

The Legged Squad Support System, LS3 (above), is another robot with the military in mind. The size of a real-life horse, the four-legged robot was designed to carry 397 lb (180 kg) of supplies and equipment alongside a squad of troops.

ODD BOTS

Make no mistake, from robot actors and apes to record-breaking runners and walkers, there are some seriously strange robots out there!

APING NATURE

RoboSimian is modeled after apes and monkeys, yet can scuttle around on the ground like a four-legged spider. The robot has 14 cameras and is able to move and handle objects using any of its four long, multijointed limbs with which it can perform pull-ups, clamber over obstacles, and swing through gaps.

BICYCLING BOT

Japanese robot MURATA BOY is a 20 in (50 cm) tall humanoid robot that can pedal a small bicycle up slopes and around corners, thanks to its array of sensors. These send back a constant stream of data about the robot's angle and position, so that MURATA BOY can detect and avoid obstacles, and even keep its balance while standing still.

EMUU

This odd-looking object is actually a robot called eMuu. It can arch its single eyebrow and change its mouth to express emotions, such as happiness, anger, or sadness.

ROBOT PERFORMER

RoboThespian (above) is a British humanoid robot with its own YouTube channel. More than 30 of these robots have appeared in plays or given talks at museums. RoboThespian can recognize human gestures and expressions and change what it says as a result.

HITCHBOT

In 2014, this strange robot with a plastic bucket for a body hitchhiked across all of Canada in 26 days. HitchBOT couldn't walk, but could talk and ask passers-by for a lift. It had a built-in GPS so it could track its own position and a camera to take snapshots of its epic journey.

FUTURE ROBOTS

Robots have come a long way, but there is plenty of progress to come. Advances in computing, sensors, software, and materials technology promise exciting times ahead. What types of robots will we see in the future?

DRIVERLESS VEHICLES

The roads of the future may be full of robotic vehicles that can communicate with each other and adjust their speed and direction to avoid crashes and traffic jams. Cars made by Google (right), Tesla, Volvo, and many other companies are being developed. The Lutz Pathfinder, the UK's first driverless car, went on trial in Milton Keynes in 2015 and 2016. This electric car uses cameras, 19 sensors, and radar to drive up to two passengers around town.

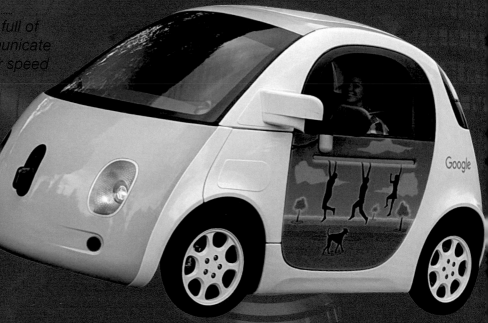

NANOBOTS

A nanometer is a billionth of a meter. Nanotechnology is the science and engineering of machines to this tiny scale, such as nanobots. These microscopic robots might be injected into the bloodstream to clean blood vessels or combat disease. Other nanobots might tackle pollution or repair machines and materials from the inside.

This artwork imagines nanobots seeking out diseased cells in human blood. Each attaches itself to a cell and injects drugs to fight the disease.

ROBOT SWARMS

Large numbers of small robots or nanobots might work together in search and rescue missions or to tackle a disaster such as an oil spill. More than one megabit or more than 1,000 kilobots at Harvard University have already been programmed to work together in a prototype robot swarm.

PERSONAL ASSISTANTS

Advances in robot movement and intelligence may allow people in the future to rely on their own personal robot pal. Such robots might be mind-controlled and act as a teacher, tutor, and babysitter when someone is young and develop with them as they grow, acting as a caregiver when the person is ill or elderly.

REPLICATING ROBOTS

Future robots may be capable of being sent to a remote location on Earth or in space and assemble themselves and other machines and robots using 3D printing and other technologies. They might be sent in advance of human explorers to the Moon, Mars, or an asteroid to build and prepare a base for a forthcoming human colony.

BUILD YOUR OWN BOT

Many people enjoy the thrill of building their own robot. Here's a very simple machine for you to make that creates random drawings as it moves across a large piece of paper. You can also fit fabric pens to the device for it to make a pattern across a piece of cloth.

YOU WILL NEED:

- a disposable cup
- a pencil
- a square of thin card stock, slightly larger than the open end of the cup
- glue
- a drawing compass
- a hot glue gun
- two AA batteries and a battery holder
- a 1.5 volt DC motor
- a slice of cork, about 5 mm thick
- a large paper clip
- three thick felt-tip pens
- masking tape
- a large sheet of plain paper

1.
Trace around the open end of the cup to create a card circle and glue it to the cup's base. Use a drawing compass to poke a hole through the card circle and cup base.

2.
Fit the batteries into the holder and replace the cover with the switch facing upward. Use the glue gun to stick the battery box to the inside of the cup.

3.

Push the battery box wires through the holes. Position the motor so that its spindle sticks out over the edge of the card circle on the opposite side to the battery box. Use the glue gun to fix the motor in place.

4.

Connect the red and black wires to the terminals on the motor to complete the electric circuit. Test that the motor is working by switching on the battery pack briefly.

5.

Use the compasses to make a hole in the middle of the edge of the piece of cork. Push the cork onto the spindle. If needs be a tight fit, so if it is too loose take it off and put a small dab of glue into the hole. Replace the cork and leave to set.

6.

Use the glue gun to fix the large paper clip to the front of the cork. Leave to set.

7.

Place the three pens around the outside of the cup and secure them with masking tape. Remove the pen lids. Place the machine on a large sheet of plain paper. Switch it on and watch your robot draw!

GLOSSARY

AGV Short for Automated Guided Vehicle. AGVs are machines that travel by themselves along a path in a factory or other building.

antenna A device, usually a long, slender aerial, that sends and receives wireless signals by radio waves.

asteroid A rocky object in space that orbits the Sun.

automata Lifelike mechanical figures made with springs, levers, gears, and other parts to mimic the actions of humans or animals.

autonomous Describes a machine that makes decisions and works by itself.

controller The part of the robot that makes decisions and tells the other parts of the robot what to do. It is usually a computer.

degrees of freedom The different directions in which a robot can move.

drive system A collection of parts in a robot that together allow the robot or parts of it to move.

drones Also known as UAVs or Unmanned Aerial Vehicles, drones are unmanned aircraft that people can control remotely.

end effector A device or tool, such as a gripping hand or a paint sprayer, connected to the end of a robot arm.

feedback Information about a robot or its surroundings that is collected from sensors and sent to a robot's controller.

friction A force between two surfaces that are rubbing or sliding across each other.

Global Positioning System (GPS) A navigation system using a series of satellites orbiting Earth to give an accurate position on Earth.

gripper A type of end effector fitted to a robot that is capable of grasping and manipulating objects.

humanoid Describes a robot that has a partial or complete humanlike appearance or one that performs humanlike actions.

hydraulics A power system found in some robots that uses liquids in cylinders.

joystick A control device made of a lever attached to a base that can be moved in several directions to guide the movement of a robot.

pneumatics A way of powering moving parts of a robot using compressed air or other gases.

microsurgery Delicate and precise medical procedures, such as the repair of blood vessels, performed by a surgeon looking through a microscope and using tiny instruments.

nanotechnology The science of building machines and robots at a scale of nanometers (billionths of a meter).

radar A system that bounces radio waves off objects to work out how far away they are.

radiation The transmission of energy as waves or rays. Radiation can be very dangerous when it takes the form of powerful energy produced by a nuclear reaction.

RoboCup An international event in which robots compete in different activities, most famously soccer matches.

sensor A device that collects information about a robot or its surroundings.

solar panels Panels containing special cells that convert sunlight into electricity.

water disrupter A tool that scrambles all the workings inside a bomb to prevent it from exploding.

FURTHER INFORMATION

Books
Adventures in STEAM: Robots by Claudia Martin (Wayland, 2018)
How to Design the World's Best Robot in 10 Simple Steps by Paul Mason (Wayland, 2017)
How to Build: Robots by Louise Derrington (Franklin Watts, 2016)

Websites
About Robots
www.about-robots.com
A nice website created by a student who is studying robotics.

The Atlantic—Robots at Work and Play
www.theatlantic.com/photo/2014/11/robots-at-work-and-play/100856
A great gallery of 30 amazing robots

Cool Robots for Kids
sites.google.com/site/coolrobotsforkids/home
This is a great website for both kids and adults who want to learn about some of the many robots of the world.

Explain that Stuff—Robots
www.explainthatstuff.com/robots.html
This really useful webpage covers how robots work and are programmed.

Robot Hall of Fame
www.robothalloffame.org/inductees.html
Check out some of the most famous fictional and real-life robots from 2003–2012.

Science Kids / Robots for Kids
www.sciencekids.co.nz/robots.html
A fun-packed website with videos of famous robots in action, games and simple craft projects, and information on how robots are programmed.

Some Interesting Facts
http://someinterestingfacts.net/facts-about-robots/
A webpage devoted to many kinds of robots and how they are becoming more like humans.

INDEX

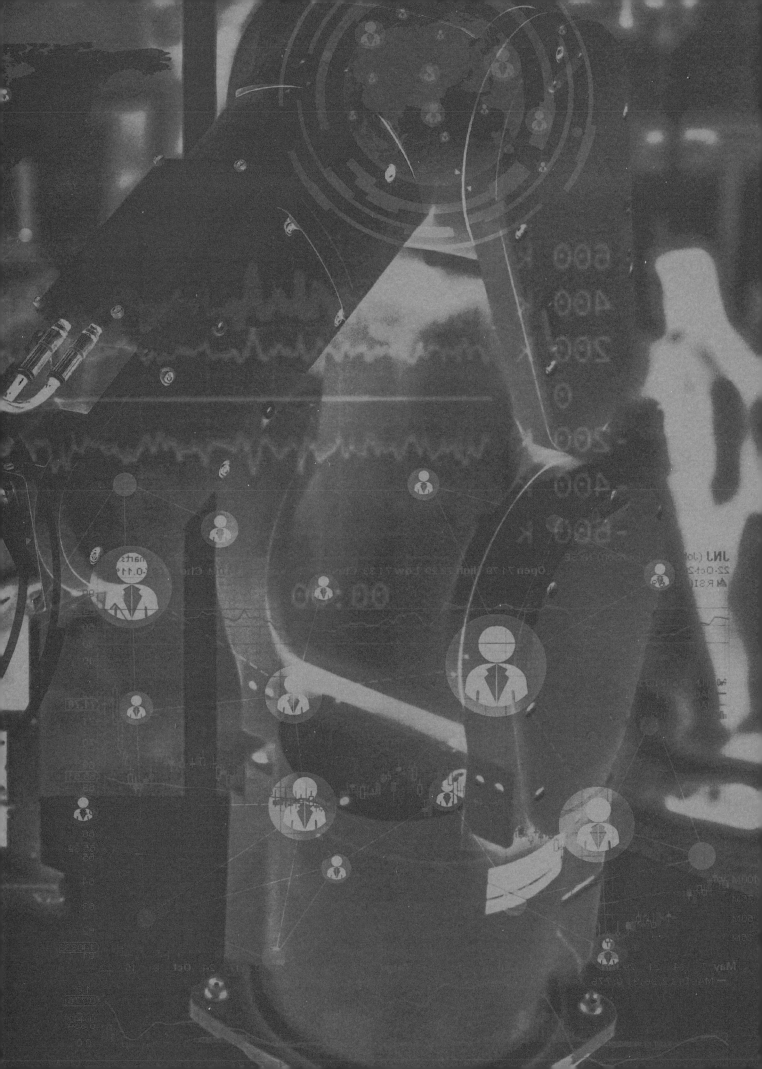